Other Places
A Kind of Alaska, Victoria Station, Family Voices

Other Works by Harold Pinter
Published by Grove Press

Other Places

Three Plays

by
HAROLD PINTER

GROVE PRESS, INC., NEW YORK

A Kind of Alaska © 1982 by Askerdale Limited
Victoria Station © 1982 by Askerdale Limited
Family Voices © 1981 by Harold Pinter

First Hardcover Edition published in 1983

First Evergreen Edition published in 1983

Library of Congress Cataloging in Publication Data

Pinter, Harold, 1930—
 Other Places.

 Contents: *A Kind of Alaska—Victoria Station—Family Voices.*
 I. Title.
PR6066.I53A6   1983   822'.914   82-24185
ISBN 0-394-53131-0
ISBN 0-394-62449-1 (paperback)

Manufactured in the United States of America

GROVE PRESS, INC., 196 West Houston Street, New York, N.Y. 10014

83 84 85 86 8 7 6 5 4 3 2 1

To Mick Goldstein

Other Places was first performed in the Cottesloe auditorium of the National Theatre, London, on 14 October 1982 with the following cast:

Family Voices

VOICE 1	Nigel Havers
VOICE 2	Anna Massey
VOICE 3	Paul Rogers

Victoria Station

CONTROLLER	Paul Rogers
DRIVER	Martin Jarvis

A Kind of Alaska

DEBORAH	Judi Dench
HORNBY	Paul Rogers
PAULINE	Anna Massey

Directed by Peter Hall
Designed by John Bury

A Kind of Alaska

A Kind of Alaska was inspired by *Awakenings* by Oliver Sacks M.D., first published in 1973 by Gerald Duckworth and Co.

In the winter of 1916–17, there spread over Europe, and subsequently over the rest of the world, an extraordinary epidemic illness which presented itself in innumerable forms – as delirium, mania, trances, coma, sleep, insomnia, restlessness, and states of Parkinsonism. It was eventually identified by the great physician Constantin von Economo and named by him *encephalitis lethargica*, or sleeping sickness.

Over the next ten years almost five million people fell victim to the disease of whom more than a third died. Of the survivors some escaped almost unscathed, but the majority moved into states of deepening illness. The worst-affected sank into singular states of 'sleep' – conscious of their surroundings but motionless, speechless, and without hope or will, confined to asylums or other institutions.

Fifty years later, with the development of the remarkable drug L-DOPA, they erupted into life once more.

Characters

DEBORAH

HORNBY

PAULINE

A woman in a white bed. Mid-forties. She sits up against high-banked pillows, stares ahead.

A table and two chairs. A window.

A man in a dark suit sits at the table. Early sixties.

The woman's eyes move. She slowly looks about her.

Her gaze passes over the man and on.
He watches her.

She stares ahead, still.

She whispers.

DEBORAH

Something is happening.

Silence.

HORNBY

Do you know me?

Silence.

Do you recognise me?

Silence.

Can you hear me?

She does not look at him.

                    DEBORAH
Are you speaking?

                    HORNBY
Yes.

Pause

Do you know who I am?

Pause

Who am I?

                    DEBORAH
No-one hears what I say. No-one is listening to me.

Pause

                    HORNBY
Do you know who I am?

Pause

Who am I?

                    DEBORAH
You are no-one.

Pause

Who is it? It is miles away. The rain is falling. I will get wet.

Pause

I can't get to sleep. The dog keeps turning about. I think he's dreaming. He wakes me up, but not himself up. He's my best dog though. I talk French.

Pause

HORNBY

I would like you to listen to me.

Pause

You have been asleep for a very long time. You have now woken up. We are here to care for you.

Pause

You have been asleep for a very long time. You are older, although you do not know that. You are still young, but older.

Pause

DEBORAH

Something is happening.

HORNBY

You have been asleep. You have awoken. Can you hear me? Do you understand me?

She looks at him for the first time.

DEBORAH

Asleep?

Pause

I do not remember that.

Pause

People have been looking at me. They have been touching me. I spoke, but I don't think they heard what I said.

Pause

What language am I speaking? I speak French, I know that. Is this French?

Pause

I've not seen Daddy today. He's funny. He makes me laugh. He runs with me. We play with balloons.

Pause

Where is he?

Pause

I think it's my birthday soon.

Pause

No, no. No, no. I sleep like other people. No more no less. Why should I? If I sleep late my mother wakes me up. There are things to do.

Pause

If I have been asleep, why hasn't Mummy woken me up?

HORNBY

I have woken you up.

DEBORAH

But I don't know you.

Pause

Where is everyone? Where is my dog? Where are my sisters? Last night Estelle was wearing my dress. But I said she could.

Pause

I am cold.

HORNBY

How old are you?

DEBORAH

I am twelve. No. I am sixteen. I am seven.

Pause

I don't know. Yes. I know. I am fourteen. I am fifteen. I'm lovely fifteen.

Pause

You shouldn't have brought me here. My mother will ask me where I've been.

Pause

You shouldn't have touched me like that. I shan't tell my mother. I shouldn't have touched you like that.

Pause

Oh Jack.

Pause

It's time I was up and about. All those dogs are making such a racket. I suppose Daddy's feeding them. Is Estelle going to marry that boy from Townley Street? The ginger boy? Pauline says he's got nothing between his ears. Thick as two planks. I've given it a good deal of rather more mature thought and I've decided she should not marry him. Tell her not to marry him. She'll listen to you.

Pause

Daddy?

HORNBY

She didn't marry him.

DEBORAH

Didn't?

Pause

It would be a great mistake. It would ruin her life.

HORNBY

She didn't marry him.

Silence.

DEBORAH

I've seen this room before. What room is this? It's not my bedroom. My bedroom has blue lilac on the walls. The sheets are soft, pretty. Mummy kisses me.

Pause

This is not my bedroom.

HORNBY

You have been in this room for a long time. You have been asleep. You have now woken up.

DEBORAH

You shouldn't have brought me here. What are you saying? Did I ask you to bring me here? Did I make eyes at you? Did I show desire for you? Did I let you peep up my skirt? Did I flash my teeth? Was I as bold as brass? Perhaps I've forgotten.

HORNBY

I didn't bring you here. Your mother and father brought you here.

DEBORAH

My father? My mother?

Pause

Did they bring me to you as a sacrifice? Did they sacrifice
me to you?

Pause

No, no. You stole me ... in the night.

Pause

Have you had your way with me?

HORNBY
I am here to take care of you.

DEBORAH
They all say that.

Pause

You've had your way with me. You made me touch you.
You stripped me. I cried ... but ... but it was my lust
made me cry. You are a devil. My lust was my own. I
kept it by me. You took it from me. Once open never closed.
Never closed again. Never closed always open. For etern-
ity. Terrible. You have ruined me.

Pause

I sound childish. Out of ... tune.

Pause

How old am I?

Pause

Eighteen?

HORNBY

No.

DEBORAH

Well then, I've no idea how old I am. Do you know?

HORNBY

Not exactly.

DEBORAH

Why not?

Pause

My sisters would know. We're very close. We love each other. We're known as the three bluebells.

Pause

Why is everything so quiet? So still? I'm in a sandbag. The sea. Is that what I hear? A long way away. Gulls. Haven't heard a gull for ages. God what a racket. Where's Pauline? She's such a mischief. I have to keep telling her not to be so witty. That's what I say. You're too witty for your own good. You're so sharp you'll cut yourself. You're too witty for your own tongue. You'll bite your own tongue off one of these days and I'll keep your tongue in a closed jar and you'll never ever ever ever be witty again.

Pause

She's all right, really. She just talks too much. Whereas Estelle is as deep as a pond. She's marvellous at crossing her legs. Sen-su-al.

Pause

This is a hotel. A hotel near the sea. Hastings? Torquay? There's more to this than meets the eye. I'm coming to that conclusion. There's something very shady about you. Pauline always says I'll end up as part of the White Slave Traffic.

Pause

Yes. This is a white tent. When I open the flap I'll step out into the Sahara Desert.

HORNBY

You've been asleep.

DEBORAH

Oh, you keep saying that! What's wrong with that? Why shouldn't I have a long sleep for a change? I need it. My body demands it. It's quite natural. I may have overslept but I didn't do it deliberately. If I had any choice in the matter I'd much prefer to be up and about. I love the morning. Why do you blame me? I was simply obeying the law of the body.

HORNBY

I know that. I'm not blaming you.

DEBORAH

Well, how long have I been asleep?

Pause

HORNBY

You have been asleep for twenty-nine years.

Silence.

DEBORAH

You mean I'm dead?

HORNBY

No.

DEBORAH

I don't feel dead.

HORNBY

You're not.

DEBORAH

But you mean I've been dead?

HORNBY

If you had been dead you wouldn't be alive now.

DEBORAH

Are you sure?

HORNBY

No-one wakes from the dead.

DEBORAH

No, I shouldn't think so.

Pause

Well, what was I doing if I wasn't dead?

HORNBY

We don't know.... what you were doing.

DEBORAH

We?

Pause

Where's my mother? My father? Estelle? Pauline?

HORNBY

Pauline is here. She's waiting to see you.

DEBORAH

She shouldn't be out at this time of night. I'm always telling her. She needs her beauty sleep. Like I do, by the way.
But of course I'm her elder sister so she doesn't listen to
me. And Estelle doesn't listen to me because she's my elder
sister. That's family life. And Jack? Where's Jack? Where's
my boyfriend? He's my boyfriend. He loves me. He loves
me. I once saw him cry. For love. Don't make him cry
again. What have you done to him? What have you done
with him? What? What? What?

HORNBY

Be calm. Don't agitate yourself.

DEBORAH

Agitate myself?

HORNBY

There's no hurry about any of this.

DEBORAH

Any of what?

HORNBY

Be calm.

DEBORAH

I am calm.

Pause

I've obviously committed a criminal offence and am now in prison. I'm quite prepared to face up to the facts. But what offence? I can't imagine what offence it could be. I mean one that would bring ... such a terrible sentence.

HORNBY

This is not a prison. You have committed no offence.

DEBORAH

But what have I done? What have I been doing? Where have I been?

HORNBY

Do you remember nothing of where you've been? Do you remember nothing ... of all that has happened to you?

DEBORAH

Nothing has happened to me. I've been nowhere.

Silence.

HORNBY

I think we should –

DEBORAH

I certainly don't want to see Pauline. People don't want to see their sisters. They're only their sisters. They're so witty. All I hear is chump chump. The side teeth. Eating everything in sight. Gold chocolate. So greedy eat it with the paper on. Munch all the ratshit on the sideboard. Someone has to polish it off. Been there for years. Statues of excrement. Wrapped in gold. I've never got used to it. Sisters are diabolical. Brothers are worse. One day I prayed I would see no-one ever again, none of them ever again. All that eating, all that wit.

Pause

HORNBY

I didn't know you had any brothers.

DEBORAH

What?

Pause

HORNBY

Come. Rest. Tomorrow ... is another day.

DEBORAH

No it isn't. No it isn't. It is not!

She smiles.

Yes, of course it is. Of course it is. Tomorrow is another day. I'd love to ask you a question.

HORNBY

Are you not tired?

DEBORAH

Tired? Not at all. I'm wide awake. Don't you think so?

HORNBY

What is the question?

DEBORAH

How did you wake me up?

Pause

Or did you not wake me up? Did I just wake up myself? All by myself? Or did you wake me with a magic wand?

HORNBY

I woke you with an injection.

DEBORAH

Lovely injection. Oh how I love it. And am I beautiful?

HORNBY

Certainly.

DEBORAH

And you are my Prince Charming. Aren't you?

Pause

Oh speak up.

Pause

Silly shit. All men are alike.

Pause

I think I love you.

                    HORNBY
No, you don't.

                    DEBORAH
Well, I'm not spoilt for choice here, am I? There's not another man in sight. What have you done with all the others? There's a boy called Peter. We play with his trains, we play.... Cowboys and Indians.... I'm a tomboy. I knock him about. But that was....

Pause

But now I've got all the world before me. All life before me. All my life before me.

Pause

I've had enough of this. Find Jack. I'll say yes. We'll have kids. I'll bake apples. I'm ready for it. No point in hanging about. Best foot forward. Mummy's motto. Bit of a cheek, I think, Mummy not coming in to say hullo, to say good-night, to tuck me up, to sing me a song, to warn me about going too far with boys. Daddy I love but he is a bit absent-minded. Thinking of other things. That's what Pauline says. She says he has a mistress in Fulham. The bitch. I mean Pauline. And she's only ... thirteen. I keep telling her I'm not prepared to tolerate her risible, her tendentious, her eclectic, her ornate, her rococo insinuations and garbled inventions. I tell her that every day of the week.

Pause

Daddy is kind and so is Mummy. We all have breakfast together every morning in the kitchen. What's happening?

Pause

HORNBY

One day suddenly you stopped.

DEBORAH

Stopped?

HORNBY

Yes.

Pause

You fell asleep and no-one could wake you. But although I use the word sleep, it was not strictly sleep.

DEBORAH

Oh, make up your mind!

Pause

You mean you thought I was asleep but I was actually awake?

HORNBY

Neither asleep nor awake.

DEBORAH

Was I dreaming?

HORNBY

Were you?

DEBORAH

Well was I? I don't know.

Pause

I'm not terribly pleased about all this. I'm going to ask a few questions in a few minutes. One of them might be: What did I look like while I was asleep, or while I was awake, or whatever it was I was? Bet you can't tell me.

HORNBY

You were quite still. Fixed. Most of the time.

DEBORAH

Show me.

Pause

Show me what I looked like.

He demonstrates a still, fixed position.
She studies him. She laughs, stops abruptly.

Most of the time? What about the rest of the time?

HORNBY

You were taken for walks twice a week. We encouraged your legs to move.

Pause

At other times you would suddenly move of your own volition very quickly, very quickly indeed, spasmodically, for short periods, and as suddenly as you began you would stop.

Pause

DEBORAH

Did you ever see ... tears ... well in my eyes?

HORNBY

No.

DEBORAH

And when I laughed ... did you laugh with me?

HORNBY

You never laughed.

DEBORAH

Of course I laughed. I have a laughing nature.

Pause

Right. I'll get up now.

He moves to her.

No! Don't! Don't be ridiculous.

She eases herself out of the bed, stands, falls.
He moves to her.

No! Don't! Don't! Don't! Don't touch me.

She stands, very slowly. He retreats, watching.
She stands still, begins to walk, in slow motion, towards him.

Let us dance.

She dances, by herself, in slow motion.

I dance.

She dances.

I've kept in practice, you know. I've been dancing in very
narrow spaces. Kept stubbing my toes and bumping my
head. Like Alice. Shall I sit here? I shall sit here.

She sits at the table. He joins her.
She touches the arms of her chair, touches the table, examines
the table.

I like tables, don't you? This is a rather beautiful table.
Any chance of a dry sherry?

HORNBY
Not yet. Soon we'll have a party for you.

DEBORAH
A party? For me? How nice. Lots of cakes and lots of booze?

HORNBY

That's right.

DEBORAH

How nice.

Pause

Well, it's nice at this table. What's the news? I suppose the war's still over?

HORNBY

It's over, yes.

DEBORAH

Oh good. They haven't started another one?

HORNBY

No.

DEBORAH

Oh good.

Pause

HORNBY

You danced in narrow spaces?

DEBORAH

Oh yes. The most crushing spaces. The most punishing spaces. That was tough going. Very difficult. Like dancing with someone dancing on your foot all the time, I mean *all* the time, on the same spot, just slam, slam, a big boot on your foot, not the most ideal kind of dancing, not by a long chalk. But sometimes the space opened and became light, sometimes it opened and I was so light, and when you feel so light you can dance till dawn and I danced till dawn night after night, night after night ... for a time ... I think ... until....

She has become aware of the figure of PAULINE, *standing in the room. She stares at her.*
PAULINE *is a woman in her early forties.*

PAULINE
Deborah.

DEBORAH *stares at her.*

Deborah. It's Pauline.

PAULINE *turns to* HORNBY.

She's looking at me.

She turns back to DEBORAH.

You're looking at me. Oh Deborah ... you haven't looked at me ... for such a long time.

Pause

I'm your sister. Do you know me?

DEBORAH *laughs shortly and turns away.*
HORNBY *stands and goes to* PAULINE.

HORNBY
I didn't call you.

PAULINE *regards him.*

Well, all right. Speak to her.

                    PAULINE
What shall I say?

                    HORNBY
Just talk to her.

                    PAULINE
Doesn't it matter what I say?

                    HORNBY
No.

                    PAULINE
I can't do her harm?

                    HORNBY
No.

                    PAULINE
Shall I tell her lies or the truth?

                    HORNBY
Both.

Pause

                    PAULINE
You're trembling.

                    HORNBY
Am I?

PAULINE

Your hand.

HORNBY

Is it?

He looks at his hand.

Trembling? Is it? Yes.

PAULINE *goes to* DEBORAH, *sits with her at the table.*

PAULINE

Debby. I've spoken to the family. Everyone was so happy.
I spoke to them all, in turn. They're away, you see. They're
on a world cruise. They deserve it. It's been so hard for
them. And Daddy's not too well, although in many respects
he's as fit as a fiddle, and Mummy.... It's a wonderful
trip. They passed through the Indian Ocean. And the
Bay of Bosphorus. Can you imagine? Estelle also ...
needed a total break. It's a wonderful trip. Quite honestly,
it's the trip of a lifetime. They've stopped off in Bangkok.
That's where I found them. I spoke to them all, in turn.
And they all send so much love to you. Especially
Mummy.

Pause

I spoke by radio telephone. Shore to ship. The captain's
cabin. Such excitement.

Pause

Tell me. Do you ... remember me?

DEBORAH *stands and walks to her bed, in slow motion.*
Very slowly she gets into the bed.
She lies against the pillows, closes her eyes.
She opens her eyes, looks at PAULINE, *beckons to her.*
PAULINE *goes to the bed.*

DEBORAH

Let me look into your eyes.

She looks deeply into PAULINE's *eyes.*

So you say you're my sister?

PAULINE

I am.

DEBORAH

Well, you've changed. A great deal. You've aged ... substantially. What happened to you?

DEBORAH *turns to* HORNBY.

What happened to her? Was it a sudden shock? I know shocks can age people overnight. Someone told me.

She turns to PAULINE.

Is that what happened to you? Did a sudden shock age you overnight?

PAULINE

No it was you –

PAULINE *looks at* HORNBY. *He looks back at her, impassive.*
PAULINE *turns back to* DEBORAH.

It was you. You were standing with a vase of flowers in your hands. You were about to put it down on the table. But you didn't put it down. You stood still, with the vase in your hands, as if you were ... fixed. I was with you, in the room. I looked into your eyes.

Pause

I said: 'Debby?'

Pause

But you remained ... quite ... still. I touched you. I said: 'Debby?' Your eyes were open. You were looking nowhere. Then you suddenly looked at me and saw me and smiled at me and put the vase down on the table.

Pause

But at the end of dinner, we were all laughing and talking, and Daddy was making jokes and making us laugh, and you said you couldn't see him properly because of the flowers in the middle of the table, where you had put them, and you stood and picked up the vase and you took it towards that little sidetable by the window, walnut, and Mummy was laughing and even Estelle was laughing and then we suddenly looked at you and you had stopped. You were standing with the vase by the sidetable, you were about to put it down, your arm was stretched towards it but you had stopped.

Pause

We went to you. We spoke to you. Mummy touched you. She spoke to you.

Pause

Then Daddy tried to take the vase from you. He could not ... wrench it from your hands. He could not ... move you from the spot. Like ... marble.

Pause

You were sixteen.

DEBORAH *turns to* HORNBY.

DEBORAH

She must be an aunt I never met. One of those distant cousins.

(*To* PAULINE:) Have you left me money in your Will? Well, I could do with it.

PAULINE

I'm Pauline.

DEBORAH

Well, if you're Pauline you've put on a remarkable amount of weight in a very short space of time. I can see you're not keeping up with your ballet classes. My God! You've grown breasts!

DEBORAH *stares at* PAULINE'*s breasts and suddenly looks down at herself.*

PAULINE

We're women.

DEBORAH

Women?

HORNBY

You're a grown woman, Deborah.

DEBORAH (*to* PAULINE:)

Is Estelle going to marry that ginger boy from Townley Street?

HORNBY

Deborah. Listen. You're not listening.

DEBORAH

To what?

HORNBY

To what your sister has been saying.

DEBORAH (*to* PAULINE:)

Are you my sister?

PAULINE

Yes. Yes.

DEBORAH

But where did you get those breasts?

PAULINE

They came about.

DEBORAH *looks down at herself.*

DEBORAH

I'm slimmer. Aren't I?

PAULINE

Yes.

DEBORAH

Yes. I'm slimmer.

Pause

I'm going to run into the sea and fall into the waves. I'm going to rummage about in all the water.

Pause

Are we going out to dinner tonight?

Pause

Where's Jack? Tongue-tied as usual. He's too shy for his own good. And Pauline's so sharp she'll cut herself. And Estelle's such a flibbertigibbet. I think she should marry that ginger boy from Townley Street and settle down before it's too late.

Pause

PAULINE

I am a widow.

DEBORAH

This woman is mad.

HORNBY

No. She's not.

Pause

She has been coming to see you regularly ... for a long time. She has suffered for you. She has never forsaken you. Nor have I.

Pause

I have been your doctor for many years. This is your sister. Your father is blind. Estelle looks after him. She never married. Your mother is dead.

Pause

It was I who took the vase from your hands. I lifted you onto this bed, like a corpse. Some wanted to bury you. I forbade it. I have nourished you, watched over you, for all this time.

Pause

I injected you and woke you up. You will ask why I did not inject you twenty-nine years ago. I'll tell you. I did not possess the appropriate fluid.

Pause

You see, you have been nowhere, absent, indifferent. It is we who have suffered.

Pause

You do see that, I'm sure. You were an extremely intelligent young girl. All opinions confirm this. Your mind has not been damaged. It was merely suspended, it took up a temporary habitation ... in a kind of Alaska. But it was not entirely static, was it? You ventured into quite remote ... utterly foreign ... territories. You kept on the move. And I charted your itinerary. Or did my best to do so. I have never let you go.

Silence.

I have never let you go.

Silence.

I have lived with you.

Pause

Your sister Pauline was twelve when you were left for dead. When she was twenty I married her. She is a widow. I have lived with you.

Silence.

DEBORAH

I want to go home.

Pause

I'm cold.

She takes PAULINE's *hand.*

Is it my birthday soon? Will I have a birthday party? Will everyone be there? Will they all come? All our friends? How old will I be?

PAULINE

You will. You will have a birthday party. And everyone
will be there. All your family will be there. All your old
friends. And we'll have presents for you. All wrapped up
... wrapped up in such beautiful paper.

DEBORAH

What presents?

PAULINE

Ah, we're not going to tell you. We're not going to tell
you that. Because they're a secret.

Pause

Think of it. Think of the thrill ... of opening them, of
unwrapping them, of taking out your presents and looking
at them.

DEBORAH

Can I keep them?

PAULINE

Of course you can keep them. They're your presents.
They're for you ... only.

DEBORAH

I might lose them.

PAULINE

No, no. We'll put them all around you in your bedroom.
We'll see that nobody else touches them. Nobody will touch
them. And we'll kiss you goodnight. And when you wake
up in the morning your presents ...

Pause

DEBORAH

I don't want to lose them.

PAULINE

They'll never be lost. Ever.

Pause

And we'll sing to you. What will we sing?

DEBORAH

What?

PAULINE

We'll sing 'Happy Birthday' to you.

Pause

DEBORAH

Now what was I going to say?

She begins to flick her cheek, as if brushing something from it.

Now what −? Oh dear, oh no. Oh dear.

Pause

Oh dear.

The flicking of her cheek grows faster.

Yes, I think they're closing in. They're closing in. They're closing the walls in. Yes.

She bows her head, flicking faster, her fingers now moving about over her face.

Oh ... well ... oooohhhhh ... oh no ... oh no ...

During the course of this speech her body becomes hunch-backed.

Let me out. Stop it. Let me out. Stop it. Stop it. Stop it. Shutting the walls on me. Shutting them down on me. So tight, so tight. Something panting, something panting. Can't see. Oh, the light is going. The light is going. They're shutting up shop. They're closing my face. Chains and padlocks. Bolting me up. Stinking. The smell. Oh my goodness, oh dear, oh my goodness, oh dear, I'm so young. It's a vice. I'm in a vice. It's at the back of my neck. Ah. Eyes stuck. Only see the shadow of the tip of my nose. Shadow of the tip of my nose. Eyes stuck.

She stops flicking abruptly, sits still. Her body straightens. She looks up. She looks at her fingers, examines them.

Nothing.

Silence.
She speaks calmly, is quite still.

Do you hear a drip?

Pause

I hear a drip. Someone's left the tap on.

Pause

I'll tell you what it is. It's a vast series of halls. With enormous interior windows masquerading as walls. The windows are mirrors, you see. And so glass reflects glass. For ever and ever.

Pause

You can't imagine how still it is. So silent I hear my eyes move.

Silence.

I'm lying in bed. People bend over me, speak to me. I want to say hullo, to have a chat, to make some inquiries. But you can't do that if you're in a vast hall of glass with a tap dripping.

Silence.
She looks at PAULINE.

I must be quite old. I wonder what I look like. But it's of no consequence. I certainly have no intention of looking into a mirror.

Pause

No.

She looks at HORNBY.

You say I have been asleep. You say I am now awake. You say I have not awoken from the dead. You say I was not dreaming then and am not dreaming now. You say I have always been alive and am alive now. You say I am a woman.

She looks at PAULINE, *then back to* HORNBY.

She is a widow. She doesn't go to her ballet classes any more. Mummy and Daddy and Estelle are on a world cruise. They've stopped off in Bangkok. It'll be my birthday soon. I think I have the matter in proportion.

Pause

Thank you.

Victoria Station

Characters

CONTROLLER

DRIVER

Lights up on office. CONTROLLER *sitting at microphone.*

CONTROLLER

274? Where are you?

Lights up on DRIVER *in car.*

CONTROLLER

274? Where are you?

Pause

DRIVER

Hullo?

CONTROLLER

274?

DRIVER

Hullo?

CONTROLLER

Is that 274?

DRIVER

That's me.

CONTROLLER

Where are you?

DRIVER

What?

Pause

CONTROLLER

I'm talking to 274? Right?

DRIVER

Yes. That's me. I'm 274. Who are you?

Pause

CONTROLLER

Who am I?

DRIVER

Yes.

CONTROLLER

Who do you think I am? I'm your office.

DRIVER .

Oh yes.

CONTROLLER

Where are you?

DRIVER

I'm cruising.

CONTROLLER

What do you mean?

Pause

Listen son. I've got a job for you. If you're in the area
I think you're in. Where are you?

DRIVER

I'm just cruising about.

CONTROLLER

Don't cruise. Stop cruising. Nobody's asking you to cruise about. What the fuck are you cruising about for?

Pause

274?

DRIVER

Hullo. Yes. That's me.

CONTROLLER

I want you to go to Victoria Station. I want you to pick up a customer coming from Boulogne. That is what I want you to do. Do you follow me? Now the question I want to ask you is this. Where are you? And don't say you're just cruising about. Just tell me if you're anywhere near Victoria Station.

DRIVER

Victoria what?

Pause

CONTROLLER

Station.

Pause

Can you help me on this?

DRIVER

Sorry?

CONTROLLER

Can you help me on this? Can you come to my aid on this?

Pause

You see, 274, I've got no-one else in the area, you see. I've only got you in the area. I think. Do you follow me?

DRIVER

I follow you, yes.

CONTROLLER

And this is a good job, 274. He wants you to take him to Cuckfield.

DRIVER

Eh?

CONTROLLER

He wants you to take him to Cuckfield. You're meeting the 10.22 from Boulogne. The European Special. His name's MacRooney. He's a little bloke with a limp. I've known him for years. You pick him up under the clock. You'll know him by his hat. He'll have a hat on with a feather in it. He'll be carrying fishing tackle. 274?

DRIVER

Hullo?

CONTROLLER

Are you hearing me?

DRIVER

Yes.

Pause

CONTROLLER

What are you doing?

DRIVER

I'm not doing anything.

CONTROLLER

How's your motor? Is your motor working?

DRIVER

Oh yes.

CONTROLLER

Your ignition's not on the blink?

DRIVER

No.

CONTROLLER

So you're sitting in a capable car?

DRIVER

I'm sitting in it, yes.

CONTROLLER

Are you in the driving seat?

Pause

Do you understand what I mean?

Pause

Do you have a driving wheel in front of you?

Pause

Because I haven't, 274. I'm just talking into this machine, trying to make some sense out of our lives. That's my function. God gave me this job. He asked me to do this job, personally. I'm your local monk, 274. I'm a monk. You follow? I lead a restricted life. I haven't got a choke and a gear lever in front of me. I haven't got a cooling system and four wheels. I'm not sitting here with wing mirrors and a jack in the boot. And if I did have a jack in the boot I'd stick it right up your arse.

Pause

Listen, 274. I've got every reason to believe that you're driving a Ford Cortina. I would very much like you to go to Victoria Station. *In* it. That means I don't want you to walk down there. I want you to drive down there. Right?

DRIVER

Everything you say is correct. This is a Ford Cortina.

CONTROLLER

Good. That's right. And you're sitting in it while we're having this conversation, aren't you?

DRIVER

That's right.

CONTROLLER

Where?

DRIVER

By the side of a park.

CONTROLLER

By the side of a park?

DRIVER

Yes.

CONTROLLER

What park?

DRIVER

A dark park.

CONTROLLER

Why is it dark?

Pause

DRIVER

That's not an easy question.

Pause

CONTROLLER

Isn't it?

DRIVER

No.

Pause

CONTROLLER

You remember this customer I was talking to you about? The one who's coming in to Victoria Station? Well, he's very keen for you to take him down to Cuckfield. He's got an old aunt down there. I've got a funny feeling she's going to leave him all her plunder. He's going down to pay his respects. He'll be in a good mood. If you play your cards right you might come out in front. Get me?

Pause

274?

DRIVER

Yes? I'm here.

CONTROLLER

Go to Victoria Station.

DRIVER

I don't know it.

CONTROLLER

You don't know it?

DRIVER

No. What is it?

Silence.

CONTROLLER

It's a station, 274.

Pause

Haven't you heard of it?

                         DRIVER

No. Never. What kind of place is it?

Pause

                         CONTROLLER

You've never heard of Victoria Station?

                         DRIVER

Never. No.

                         CONTROLLER

It's a famous station.

                         DRIVER

Well, I honestly don't know what I've been doing all these
years.

                         CONTROLLER

What have you been doing all these years?

                         DRIVER

Well, I honestly don't know.

Pause

                         CONTROLLER

All right 274. Report to the office in the morning. 135?
Where are you? 135? Where are you?

                         DRIVER

Don't leave me.

CONTROLLER

What? Who's that?

DRIVER

It's me. 274. Please. Don't leave me.

CONTROLLER

135? Where are you?

DRIVER

Don't have anything to do with 135. He's not your man.
He'll lead you into blind alleys by the dozen. They all will.
Don't leave me. I'm your man. I'm the only one you can
trust.

Pause

CONTROLLER

Do I know you, 274? Have we met?

Pause

Well, it'll be nice to meet you in the morning. I'm really
looking forward to it. I'll be sitting here with my cat o'nine
tails, son. And you know what I'm going to do with it?
I'm going to tie you up bollock naked to a butcher's table
and I'm going to flog you to death all the way to Crystal
Palace.

DRIVER

That's where I am! I knew I knew the place.

Pause

I'm sitting by a little dark park underneath Crystal Palace. I can see the Palace. It's silhouetted against the sky. It's a wonderful edifice, isn't it?

Pause

My wife's in bed. Probably asleep. And I've got a little daughter.

CONTROLLER

Oh, you've got a little daughter?

Pause

DRIVER

Yes, I think that's what she is.

CONTROLLER

Report to the office at 9 a.m. 135? Where are you? Where the fuck is 135? 246? 178? 101? Will somebody help me? Where's everyone gone? I've got a good job going down to Cuckfield. Can anyone hear me?

DRIVER

I can hear you.

CONTROLLER

Who's that?

DRIVER

274. Here. Waiting. What do you want me to do?

CONTROLLER

You want to know what I want you to do?

DRIVER

Oh by the way, there's something I forgot to tell you.

CONTROLLER

What is it?

DRIVER

I've got a P.O.B.

CONTROLLER

You've got a P.O.B.?

DRIVER

Yes. That means passenger on board.

CONTROLLER

I know what it means, 274. It means you've got a passenger on board.

DRIVER

That's right.

CONTROLLER

You've got a passenger on board sitting by the side of a park?

DRIVER

That's right.

CONTROLLER

Did I book this job?

DRIVER

No, I don't think you came into it.

CONTROLLER

Well, where does he want to go?

DRIVER

He doesn't want to go anywhere. We just cruised about for a bit and then we came to rest.

CONTROLLER

In Crystal Palace?

DRIVER

Not *in* the Palace.

CONTROLLER

Oh, you're not *in* the Palace?

DRIVER

No. I'm not right inside it.

CONTROLLER

I think you'll find the Crystal Palace burnt down years ago, old son. It burnt down in the Great Fire of London.

Pause

DRIVER

Did it?

CONTROLLER

274?

DRIVER

Yes. I'm here.

CONTROLLER

Drop your passenger. Drop your passenger at his chosen destination and proceed to Victoria Station. Otherwise I'll destroy you bone by bone. I'll suck you in and blow you out in little bubbles. I'll chew your stomach out with my own teeth. I'll eat all the hair off your body. You'll end up looking like a pipe cleaner. Get me?

Pause

274?

Pause

You're beginning to obsess me. I think I'm going to die. I'm alone in this miserable freezing fucking office and nobody loves me. Listen, pukeface –

DRIVER

Yes?

Pause

CONTROLLER

135? 135? Where are you?

DRIVER

Don't have anything to do with 135. They're all blood-suckers. I'm the only one you can trust.

Pause.

CONTROLLER

You know what I've always dreamed of doing? I've always had this dream of having a holiday in sunny Barbados. I'm thinking of taking this holiday at the end of this year, 274. I'd like you to come with me. To Barbados. Just the two of us. I'll take you snorkelling. We can swim together in the blue Caribbean.

Pause

In the meantime, though, why don't you just pop back to the office now and I'll make you a nice cup of tea? You can tell me something about your background, about your ambitions and aspirations. You can tell me all about your little hobbies and pastimes. Come over and have a nice cup of tea, 274.

DRIVER

I'd love to but I've got a passenger on board.

CONTROLLER

Put your passenger on to me. Let me have a word with him.

DRIVER

I can't. She's asleep on the back seat.

CONTROLLER

She?

DRIVER

Can I tell you a secret?

CONTROLLER

Please do.

DRIVER

I think I've fallen in love. For the first time in my life.

CONTROLLER

Who have you fallen in love with?

DRIVER

With this girl on the back seat. I think I'm going to keep her for the rest of my life. I'm going to stay in this car with her for the rest of my life. I'm going to marry her in this car. We'll die together in this car.

Pause

CONTROLLER

So you've found true love at last, eh, 274?

DRIVER

Yes. I've found true love at last.

CONTROLLER

So you're a happy man now then, are you?

DRIVER

I'm very happy. I've never known such happiness.

CONTROLLER

Well, I'd like to be the first to congratulate you, 274. I'd like to extend my sincere felicitations to you.

DRIVER

Thank you very much.

CONTROLLER

Don't mention it. I'll have to make a note in my diary not to forget your Golden Wedding, won't I? I'll bring along some of the boys to drink your health. Yes, I'll bring along some of the boys. We'll all have a few jars and a bit of a sing-song.

Pause

274?

Pause

DRIVER

Hullo. Yes. It's me.

CONTROLLER

Listen. I've been thinking. I've decided that what I'd like to do now is to come down there and shake you by the hand straightaway. I'm going to shut this little office and I'm going to jump into my old car and I'm going to pop down to see you, to shake you by the hand. All right?

DRIVER

Fine. But what about this man coming off the train at Victoria Station – the 10.22 from Boulogne?

CONTROLLER

He can go and fuck himself.

DRIVER

I see.

CONTROLLER

No, I'd like to meet your lady friend, you see. And we can have a nice celebration. Can't we? So just stay where you are. Right?

Pause

Right?

Pause

274?

                    DRIVER
Yes?

                    CONTROLLER
Don't move. Stay exactly where you are. I'll be right with
you.

                    DRIVER
No, I won't move.

Silence.

I'll be here.

Light out in office.
The DRIVER *sits still.*
Light out in car.

Family Voices

Characters

VOICE 1, *a young man*

VOICE 2, *a woman*

VOICE 3, *a man*

Family Voices was first broadcast on BBC Radio 3 on 22nd January 1981.

The cast was as follows:

VOICE 1   Michael Kitchen
VOICE 2   Peggy Ashcroft
VOICE 3   Mark Dignam

Director Peter Hall

Family Voices was subsequently presented in a 'platform performance' by the National Theatre, London, on 13 February 1981. Cast and director were the same. The decor was by John Bury.

I am having a very nice time.

The weather is up and down, but surprisingly warm, on the whole, more often than not.

I hope you're feeling well, and not as peaky as you did, the last time I saw you.

No, you didn't feel peaky, you felt perfectly well, you simply looked peaky.

Do you miss me?

I am having a very nice time and I hope you are glad of that.

At the moment I am dead drunk.

I had five pints in The Fishmongers Arms tonight, followed by three double scotches, and literally rolled home.

When I say home I can assure you that my room is extremely pleasant. So is the bathroom. Extremely pleasant. I have some very pleasant baths indeed in the bathroom. So does everybody else in the house. They all lie quite naked in the bath and have very pleasant baths indeed. All the people in the house go about saying what a superb bath and bathroom the one we share is, they go about telling literally everyone they meet what lovely baths you can get in this place, more or less unparalleled, to put it bluntly.

It's got a lot to do with the landlady, who is a Mrs Withers, a person who turns out to be an utterly charming person, of impeccable credentials.

When I said I was drunk I was of course making a joke.

I bet you laughed.

Mother?

Did you get the joke? You know I never touch alcohol.

I like being in this enormous city, all by myself. I expect to make friends in the not too distant future.

I expect to make girlfriends too.

I expect to meet a very nice girl. Having met her, I shall bring her home to meet my mother.

I like walking in this enormous city, all by myself. It's fun to know no-one at all. When I pass people in the street they don't realise that I don't know them from Adam. They know other people and even more other people know them, so they naturally think that even if I don't know them I know the other people. So they look at me, they try to catch my eye, they expect me to speak. But as I do not know them I do not speak. Nor do I ever feel the slightest temptation to do so.

You see, mother, I am not lonely, because all that has ever happened to me is with me, keeps me company; my childhood, for example, through which you, my mother, and he, my father, guided me.

I get on very well with my landlady, Mrs Withers. She tells me I am her solace. I have a drink with her at lunchtime and another one at teatime and then take her for a couple in the evening at The Fishmongers Arms.

She was in the Women's Air Force in the Second World War. Don't drop a bollock, Charlie, she's fond of saying, Call him Flight Sergeant and he'll be happy as a pig in shit.

You'd really like her, mother.

I think it's dawn. I can see it coming up. Another day. A day I warmly welcome. And so I shall end this letter to you, my dear mother, with my love.

VOICE 2

Darling. Where are you? The flowers are wonderful here. The blooms. You so loved them. Why do you never write?

I think of you and wonder how you are. Do you ever think of me? Your mother? Ever? At all?

Have you changed your address?

Have you made friends with anyone? A nice boy? Or a nice girl?

There are so many nice boys and nice girls about. But please don't get mixed up with the other sort. They can land you in such terrible trouble. And you'd hate it so. You're so scrupulous, so particular.

I often think that I would love to live happily ever after with you and your young wife. And she would be such a

lovely wife to you and I would have the occasional dinner
with you both. A dinner I would be quite happy to cook
myself, should you both be tired after your long day, as
I'm sure you will be.

I sometimes walk the cliff path and think of you. I think
of the times you walked the cliff path, with your father,
with cheese sandwiches. Didn't you? You both sat on the
clifftop and ate my cheese sandwiches together. Do you
remember our little joke? Munch, munch. We had a damn
good walk, your father would say. You mean you had a
good munch munch, I would say. And you would both
laugh.

Darling. I miss you. I gave birth to you. Where are you?

I wrote to you three months ago, telling you of your
father's death. Did you receive my letter?

VOICE I

I'm not at all sure that I like the people in this house,
apart from Mrs Withers and her daughter, Jane. Jane is
a schoolgirl who works hard at her homework.

She keeps her nose to the grindstone. This I find impres-
sive. There's not too much of that about these days. But
I'm not so sure about the other people in this house.

One is an old man.

The one who is an old man retires early. He is bald.

The other is a woman who wears red dresses.

The other one is another man.

He is big. He is much bigger than the other man. His hair is black. He has black eyebrows and black hair on the back of his hands.

I ask Mrs Withers about them but she will talk of nothing but her days in the Women's Air Force in the Second World War.

I have decided that Jane is not Mrs Withers' daughter but her grand-daughter. Mrs Withers is seventy. Jane is fifteen. That I am convinced is the truth.

At night I hear whispering from the other rooms and do not understand it. I hear steps on the stairs but do not dare go out to investigate.

VOICE 2

As your father grew closer to his death he spoke more and more of you, with tenderness and bewilderment. I consoled him with the idea that you had left home to make him proud of you. I think I succeeded in this. One of his last sentences was: Give him a slap on the back from me. Give him a slap on the back from me.

VOICE 1

I have made a remarkable discovery. The old man who is bald and who retires early is named Withers. Benjamin Withers. Unless it is simply a coincidence it must mean that he is a relation.

I asked Mrs Withers what the truth of this was. She poured herself a gin and looked at it before she drank it.

Then she looked at me and said: You are my little pet.
I've always wanted a little pet but I've never had one and
now I've got one.

Sometimes she gives me a cuddle, as if she were my mother.

But I haven't forgotten that I have a mother and that you
are my mother.

VOICE 2

Sometimes I wonder if you remember that you have a
mother.

VOICE 1

Something has happened. The woman who wears red
dresses stopped me and asked me into her room for a cup of
tea. I went into her room. It was far bigger than I had
expected, with sofas and curtains and veils and shrouds and
rugs and soft material all over the walls, dark blue. Jane was
sitting on a sofa doing her homework, by the look of it.
I was invited to sit on the same sofa. Tea had already
been made and stood ready, in a china teaset, of a most
elegant design. I was given a cup. So was Jane, who smiled
at me. I haven't introduced myself, the woman said, my
name is Lady Withers. Jane sipped her tea with her legs up
on the sofa. Her stockinged toes came to rest on my thigh.
It wasn't the biggest sofa in the world. Lady Withers sat
opposite us on a substantially bigger sofa. Her dress, I
decided, wasn't red but pink. Jane was in green, apart from
her toes, which were clad in black. Lady Withers asked me
about you, mother. She asked me about my mother. I said,
with absolute conviction, that you were the best mother in
the world. She asked me to call her Lally. And to call
Jane Jane. I said I did call Jane Jane. Jane gave me a

bun. I think it was a bun. Lady Withers bit into her bun.
Jane bit into her bun, her toes now resting on my lap. Lady
Withers seemed to be enjoying her bun, on her sofa. She
finished it and picked up another. I had never seen so many
buns. One quick glance told me they were perched on
cakestands, all over the room. Lady Withers went through
her second bun with no trouble at all and was at once on
to another. Jane, on the other hand, chewed almost dream-
ily at her bun and when a currant was left stranded on
her upper lip she licked it off, without haste. I could
not reconcile this with the fact that her toes were quite
restless, even agitated. Her mouth, eating, was measured,
serene; her toes, not eating, were agitated, highly strung,
some would say hysterical. My bun turned out to be rock
solid. I bit into it, it jumped out of my mouth and bounced
into my lap. Jane's feet caught it. It calmed her toes down.
She juggled the bun, with some expertise, along them. I
recalled that, in an early exchange between us, she had
told me she wanted to be an acrobat.

VOICE 2

Darling. Where are you? Why do you never write? Nobody knows your whereabouts. Nobody knows if you are
alive or dead. Nobody can find you. Have you changed
your name?

If you are alive you are a monster. On his deathbed your
father cursed you. He cursed me too, to tell the truth. He
cursed everyone in sight. Except that you were not in sight.
I do not blame you entirely for your father's ill humour,
but your absence and silence were a great burden on him,
a weariness to him. He died in lamentation and oath. Was
that your wish? Now I am alone, apart from Millie, who
sometimes comes over from Dover. She is some consola-

tion. Her eyes well with tears when she speaks of you, your dear sister's eyes well with tears. She has made a truly happy marriage and has a lovely little boy. When he is older he will want to know where his uncle is. What shall we say?

Or perhaps you will arrive here in a handsome new car, one day, in the not too distant future, in a nice new suit, quite out of the blue, and hold me in your arms.

VOICE I

Lady Withers stood up. As Jane is doing her homework, she said, perhaps you would care to leave and come again another day. Jane withdrew her feet, my bun clasped between her two big toes. Yes of course, I said, unless Jane would like me to help her with her homework. No thank you, said Lady Withers, I shall help her with her homework.

What I didn't say is that I am thinking of offering myself out as a tutor. I consider that I would make an excellent tutor, to the young, in any one of a number of subjects. Jane would be an ideal pupil. She possesses a true love of learning. That is the sense of her one takes from her every breath, her every sigh and exhalation. When she turns her eyes upon you you see within her eyes, raw, untutored, unexercised but willing, a deep love of learning.

These are midnight thoughts, mother, although the time is ten twenty-three, precisely.

VOICE 2

Darling?

While I was lying in my bath this afternoon, thinking on these things, there was apparently a knock on the front door. The man with black hair apparently opened the door. Two women stood on the doorstep. They said they were my mother and my sister, and asked for me. He denied knowledge of me. No, he had not heard of me. No, there was no-one of that name resident. This was a family house, no strangers admitted. No, they got on very well, thank you very much, without intruders. I suggest, he said, that you both go back to where you come from, and stop bothering innocent hardworking people with your slanders and your libels, these all too predictable excrescences of the depraved mind at the end of its tether. I can smell your sort a mile off and I am quite prepared to put you both on a charge of malicious mischief, insulting behaviour and vagabondage, in other words wandering around on doorsteps knowingly, without any visible means of support. So piss off out of it before I call a copper.

I was lying in my bath when the door opened. I thought I had locked it. My name's Riley, he said, How's the bath? Very nice, I said. You've got a wellknit yet slender frame, he said, I thought you only a snip, I never imagined you would be as wellknit and slender as I now see you are. Oh thank you, I said. Don't thank me, he said, It's God you have to thank. Or your mother. I've just dismissed a couple of imposters at the front door. We'll get no more shit from that quarter. He then sat on the edge of the bath and recounted to me what I've just recounted to you.

It interests me that my father wasn't bothered to make the trip.

VOICE 2

I hear your father's step on the stair. I hear his cough. But his step and his cough fade. He does not open the door.

Sometimes I think I have always been sitting like this. I sometimes think I have always been sitting like this, alone by an indifferent fire, curtains closed, night, winter.

You see, I have my thoughts too. Thoughts no-one else knows I have, thoughts none of my family ever knew I had. But I write of them to you now, wherever you are.

What I mean is that when, for example, I was washing your hair, with the most delicate shampoo, and rinsing, and then drying your hair so gently with my soft towel, so that no murmur came from you, of discomfort or unease, and then looked into your eyes, and saw you look into mine, knowing that you wanted no-one else, no-one at all, knowing that you were entirely happy in my arms, I knew also, for example, that I was at the same time sitting by an indifferent fire, alone in winter, in eternal night without you.

VOICE 1

Lady Withers plays the piano. They were sitting, the three women, about the room. About the room were bottles of a vin rosé, of a pink I shall never forget. They sipped their wine from such lovely glass, an elegance of gesture and grace I thought long dead. Lady Withers wore a necklace around her alabaster neck, a neck amazingly young. She played Schumann. She smiled at me. Mrs Withers and Jane smiled at me. I took a seat. I took it and sat in it. I am in it. I will never leave it.

Oh mother, I have found my home, my family. Little did
I ever dream I could know such happiness.

VOICE 2
Perhaps I should forget all about you. Perhaps I should
curse you as your father cursed you. Oh I pray, I pray your
life is a torment to you. I wait for your letter begging me
to come to you. I'll spit on it.

VOICE 1
Mother, mother, I've had the most unpleasant, the most
mystifying encounter, with the man who calls himself Mr
Withers. Will you give me your advice?

Come in here, son, he called. Look sharp. Don't mess
about. I haven't got all night. I went in. A jug. A basin. A
bicycle.

You know where you are? he said. You're in my room. It's
not Euston station. Get me? It's a true oasis.

This is the only room in this house where you can pick
up a caravanserai to all points West. Compris? Com-
prende? Get me? Are you prepared to follow me down the
mountain? Look at me. My name's Withers. I'm there or
thereabouts. Follow? Embargo on all duff terminology.
With me? Embargo on all things redundant. All areas in
that connection verboten. You're in a diseaseridden land,
boxer. Keep your weight on all the left feet you can lay
your hands on. Keep dancing. The old foxtrot is the classi-
cal response but that's not the response I'm talking about.
Nor am I talking about the other response. Up the slaves.
Get me? This is a place of creatures, up and down stairs.
Creatures of the rhythmic splits, the rhythmic sideswipes,

the rums and roulettes, the macaroni tatters, the dumplings
in jam mayonnaise, a catapulting ordure of gross and ram-
shackle shenanigans, openended paraphernalia. Follow
me? It all adds up. It's before you and behind you. I'm the
only saviour of the grace you find yourself wanting in.
Mind how you go. Look sharp. Get my drift? Don't let
it get too mouldy. Watch the mould. Get the feel of it,
sonny, get the density. Look at me.

And I did.

VOICE 2

I am ill.

VOICE 1

It was like looking into a pit of molten lava, mother. One
look was enough for me.

VOICE 2

Come to me.

VOICE 1

I joined Mrs Withers for a Campari and soda in the kitchen.
She spoke of her youth. I was a right titbit, she said. I
was like a piece of plum duff. They used to come from
miles to try their luck. I fell head over heels with a man
in the Fleet Air Arm. He adored me. They had him
murdered because they didn't want us to know happiness.
I could have married him and had tons of sons. But oh
no. He went down with his ship. I heard it on the wireless.

VOICE 2

I wait for you.

VOICE I

Later that night Riley and I shared a cup of cocoa in his quarters. I like slender lads, Riley said. Slender but strong. I've never made any secret of it. But I've had to restrain myself, I've had to keep a tight rein on my inclinations. That's because my deepest disposition is towards religion. I've always been a deeply religious man. You can imagine the tension this creates in my soul. I walk about in a constant state of spiritual, emotional, psychological and physical tension. It's breathtaking, the discipline I'm called upon to exert. My lust is unimaginably violent but it goes against my best interests, which are to keep on the right side of God. I'm a big man, as you see, I could crush a slip of a lad such as you to death, I mean the death that is love, the death I understand love to be. But meet it is that I keep those desires shackled in handcuffs and leg-irons. I'm good at that sort of thing because I'm a policeman by trade. And I'm highly respected. I'm highly respected both in the force and in church. The only place where I'm not highly respected is in this house. They don't give a shit for me here. Although I've always been a close relation. Of a sort. I'm a fine tenor but they never invite me to sing. I might as well be living in the middle of the Sahara desert. There are too many women here, that's the trouble. And it's no use talking to Baldy. He's well away. He lives in another area, best known to himself. I like health and strength and intelligent conversation. That's why I took a fancy to you, chum, apart from the fact that I fancy you. I've got no-one to talk to. These women treat me like a leper. Even though I am a relation. Of a sort.

What relation?

Is Lady Withers Jane's mother or sister?

If either is the case why isn't Jane called Lady Jane Withers? Or perhaps she is. Or perhaps neither is the case? Or perhaps Mrs Withers is actually the Honourable Mrs Withers? But if that is the case what does that make Mr Withers? And which Withers is he anyway? I mean what relation is he to the rest of the Witherses? And who is Riley?

But if you find me bewildered, anxious, confused, uncertain and afraid, you also find me content. My life possesses shape. The house has a very warm atmosphere, as you have no doubt gleaned. And as you have no doubt noted from my account I talk freely to all its inhabitants, with the exception of Mr Withers, to whom no-one talks, to whom no-one refers, with evidently good reason. But I rarely leave the house. No-one seems to leave the house. Riley leaves the house but rarely. He must be a secret policeman. Jane continues to do a great deal of homework while not apparently attending any school. Lady Withers never leaves the house. She has guests. She receives guests. Those are the steps I hear on the stairs at night.

VOICE 3

I know your mother has written to you to tell you that I am dead. I am not dead. I am very far from being dead, although lots of people have wished me dead, from time immemorial, you especially. It is you who have prayed for my death, from time immemorial. I have heard your prayers. They ring in my ears. Prayers yearning for my death. But I am not dead.

Well, that is not entirely true, not entirely the case. I'm lying. I'm leading you up the garden path, I'm playing about, I'm having my bit of fun, that's what. Because

I am dead. As dead as a doornail. I'm writing to you from my grave. A quick word for old time's sake. Just to keep in touch. An old hullo out of the dark. A last kiss from Dad.

I'll probably call it a day after this canter. Not much more to say. All a bit of a sweat. Why am I taking the trouble? Because of you, I suppose, because you were such a loving son. I'm smiling, as I lie in this glassy grave.

Do you know why I use the word glassy? Because I can see out of it.

Lots of love, son. Keep up the good work.

There's only one thing bothers me, to be quite frank. While there is, generally, absolute silence everywhere, absolute silence throughout all the hours, I still hear, occasionally, a dog barking. I hear this dog. Oh, it frightens me.

VOICE I

They have decided on a name for me. They call me Bobo. Good morning, Bobo, they say, or, See you in the morning, Bobo, or, Don't drop a goolie, Bobo, or, Don't forget the diver, Bobo, or, Keep your eye on the ball, Bobo, or, Keep this side of the tramlines, Bobo, or, How's the lead in your pencil, Bobo, or, How's tricks in the sticks, Bobo, or, Don't get too much gum in your gumboots, Bobo.

The only person who does not call me Bobo is the old man. He calls me nothing. I call him nothing. I don't see him. He keeps to his room. I don't go near it. He is old and will die soon.

VOICE 2

The police are looking for you. You may remember that
you are still under twenty-one. They have issued your
precise description to all the organs. They will not rest,
they assure me, until you are found. I have stated my
belief that you are in the hands of underworld figures who
are using you as a male prostitute. I have declared in my
affidavit that you have never possessed any strength of
character whatsoever and that you are palpably susceptible
to even the most blatant form of flattery and blandishment.
Women were your downfall, even as a nipper. I haven't forgotten Françoise the French maid or the woman who
masqueraded under the title of governess, the infamous
Miss Carmichael. You will be found, my boy, and no mercy
will be shown to you.

VOICE 1

I'm coming back to you, mother, to hold you in my arms.

I am coming home.

I am coming also to clasp my father's shoulder. Where is
the old boy? I'm longing to have a word with him. Where
is he? I've looked in all the usual places, including the old
summerhouse, but I can't find him. Don't tell me he's left
home at his age? That would be inexpressibly skittish a
gesture, on his part. What have you done with him,
mother?

VOICE 2

I'll tell you what, my darling. I've given you up as a very
bad job. Tell me one last thing. Do you think the word
love means anything?

VOICE 1

I am on my way back to you. I am about to make the
journey back to you. What will you say to me?

VOICE 3

I have so much to say to you. But I am quite dead. What
I have to say to you will never be said.

OTHER GROVE PRESS DRAMA AND THEATER PAPERBACKS

B415   ARDEN, JOHN / John Arden Plays: One (Sergeant Musgrave's Dance, The Workhouse Donkey, Armstrong's Last Goodnight) / $4.95

B423   AYCKBOURN, ALAN / Absurd Person Singular, Absent Friends, Bedroom Farce: Three Plays / $3.95

E425   BARAKA, IMAMU AMIRI (LEROI JONES) / The Baptism and The Toilet: Two Plays / $3.95

E670   BARAKA, IMAMU AMIRI (LEROI JONES) / The System of Dante's Hell, The Dead Lecturer and Tales / $4.95

E96   BECKETT, SAMUEL / Endgame / $2.95

E318   BECKETT, SAMUEL / Happy Days / $2.95

E777   BECKETT, SAMUEL / Rockaby and Other Works / $3.95

E33   BECKETT, SAMUEL / Waiting for Godot / $2.95 [See also Nine plays of the Modern Theater, Harold Clurman, ed., E773 / $11.95]

B411   BEHAN, BRENDAN / The Complete Plays (The Hostage, The Quare Fellow, Richard's Cork Leg, Three One Act Plays for Radio) / $4.95

E784   BENTLEY, ERIC / Are You Now Or Have You Ever Been and Other Plays (The Recantation of Galileo Galilei; From the Memoirs of Pontius Pilate) / $12.50

B312   BRECHT, BERTOLT / The Caucasian Chalk Circle / $2.95

B119   BRECHT, BERTOLT / Edward II: A Chronicle Play / $1.95

B120   BRECHT, BERTOLT / Galileo / $2.45

B117   BRECHT, BERTOLT / The Good Woman of Setzuan / $2.95

B80   BRECHT, BERTOLT / The Jewish Wife and Other Short Plays (In Search of Justice, The Informer, The Elephant Calf, The Measures Taken, The Exception and the Rule, Salzburg Dance of Death) / $1.95

B414   BRECHT, BERTOLT / The Mother / $2.95

B333	BRECHT, BERTOLT / The Threepenny Opera / $2.45
E773	CLURMAN, HAROLD, ed. / Nine Plays of the Modern Theater (Waiting for Godot by Samuel Beckett, The Visit by Friedrich Durrenmatt, Tango by Slawomir Mrozek, The Caucasion Chalk Circle by Bertolt Brecht, The Balcony by Jean Genet, Rhinoceros by Eugene Ionesco, American Buffalo by David Mamet, The Birthday Party by Harold Pinter, and Rosencrantz and Guildenstern Are Dead by Tom Stoppard) / $11.95
E742	COWARD, NOEL / Three Plays (Private Lives, Hay Fever, Blithe Spirit) / $4.50
E159	DELANEY, SHELAGH / A Taste of Honey / $3.95
E344	DURRENMATT, FRIEDRICH. / The Visit / $4.95
E223	GELBER, JACK / The Connection / $3.95
E130	GENET, JEAN / The Balcony / $4.95 [See also Nine Plays of the Modern Theater, Harold Clurman, ed., E773 / $11.95]
E208	GENET, JEAN / The Blacks: A Clown Show / $5.95
E577	GENET, JEAN / The Maids and Deathwatch: Two Plays / $5.95
B382	GENET, JEAN / Querelle / $2.95
E374	GENET, JEAN / The Screens / $4.95
E677	GRIFFITHS, TREVOR / The Comedians / $3.95
E769	HARWOOD, RONALD / The Dresser / $5.95
B154	HOCHHUTH, ROLF / The Deputy / $4.95
E734	HODGSON, JOHN and RICHARDS, ERNEST / Improvisation / $4.95
B417	INGE, WILLIAM / Four Plays by William Inge (Come Back, Little Sheba; Picnic; Bus Stop; The Dark at the Top of the Stairs) / $3.95
E456	IONESCO, EUGENE / Exit the King / $2.95
E101	IONESCO, EUGENE / Four Plays (The Bald Soprano, The Lesson, The Chairs, Jack, or The Submission) / $4.95
E613	IONESCO, EUGENE / Killing Game / $2.95
E614	IONESCO, EUGENE / Macbett / $2.95
E259	IONESCO, EUGENE / Rhinoceros and Other Plays (The Leader, The Future Is in Eggs) / $4.95
E485	IONESCO, EUGENE / A Stroll in the Air and Frenzy for Two or More: Two Plays / $2.45

E697   MAMET, DAVID / American Buffalo / $3.95
E709   MAMET, DAVID / A Life in the Theatre / $3.95
E778   MAMET, DAVID / Lakeboat / $4.95
E712   MEMET, DAVID / Sexual Perversity in Chicago and The Duck
           Variations: Two Plays / $3.95
E716   MAMET, DAVID / The Water Engine and Mr. Happiness: Two
           Plays / $3.95
B107   MOON, SAMUEL, ed. / One Act: Eleven Short Plays of the
           Modern Theater (Miss Julie by August Strindberg, Purgatory by
           William Butler Yeats, The Man With the Flower in His Mouth by
           Luigi Pirandello, Pullman Car Hiawatha by Thornton Wilder, Hello
           Out There by William Saroyan, 27 Wagons Full of Cotton by
           Tennessee Williams, Bedtime Story by Sean O'Casey, Cecile by
           Jean Anouilh, This Music Crept By Me Upon the Waters by
           Archibald MacLeish, A Memory of Two Mondays by Arthur Miller,
           The Chairs by Eugene Ionesco) / $7.95
B429   ODETS, CLIFFORD / Six Plays of Clifford Odets (Waiting for Lefty,
           Awake and Sing, Golden Boy, Rocket to the Moon, Till the Day I
           Die, Paradise Lost) / $7.95
B400   ORTON, JOE / The Complete Plays (The Ruffian on the Stair, The
           Good and Faithful Servant, The Erpingham Camp, Funeral
           Games, Loot, What the Butler Saw, Entertaining Mr. Sloane) /
           $6.95
E724   PINTER, HAROLD / Betrayal / $3.95
E315   PINTER, HAROLD / The Birthday Party and The Room: Two Plays
           / $3.95
B402   PINTER, HAROLD / Complete Works: One (The Birthday Party,
           The Room, The Dumb Waiter, A Slight Ache, A Night Out, The
           Black and White, The Examination) / $6.95
B403   PINTER, HAROLD / Complete Works: Two (The Caretaker, Night
           School, The Dwarfs, The Collection, The Lover, Five Revue
           Sketches) / $6.95
B410   PINTER, HAROLD / Complete Works: Three (Landscape, Silence,
           The Basement, Six Revue Sketches, Tea Party [play], Tea Party
           [short story], Mac) / $6.95
E791   PINTER, HAROLD / Family Voices: A Play for Radio / $7.95
E411   PINTER, HAROLD / The Homecoming / $4.95

E764   PINTER, HAROLD / The Hothouse / $4.95
E744   POMERANCE, BERNARD / The Elephant Man / $4.25
B467   RATTIGAN, TERENCE / Plays: One (French Without Tears; The Winslow Boy; The Browning Version; Harlequinade) / $5.95
E497   SHAW, ROBERT / The Man in the Glass Booth / $2.95
E757   SHAWN, WALLACE / Marie and Bruce / $4.95
E763   SHAWN, WALLACE, and GREGORY, ANDRE / My Dinner with Andre / $5.95
E684   STOPPARD, TOM / Dirty Linen and New-Found-Land: Two Plays /$2.95
E626   STOPPARD, TOM / Jumpers / $2.95
E726   STOPPARD, TOM / Night and Day / $3.95
B319   STOPPARD, TOM / Rosencrantz and Guildenstern Are Dead / $2.95
E62   WALEY, ARTHUR, tr. and ed. / The Nō Plays of Japan / $5.95

Critical studies

E127   ARTAUD, ANTONIN / The Theater and Its Double / $3.95
E743   BENTLEY, ERIC / The Brecht Commentaries / $9.50
E819   BERLIN, NORMAND / Eugene O'Neill / $8.95
E794   CARSON, NEIL / Arthur Miller / $6.95
E441   COHN, RUBY, ed. / Casebook on Waiting for Godot / $4.95
E793   COHN, RUBY / New American Dramatists: 1960-1980 / $7.95
E797   DUKORE, BERNARD / Harold Pinter / $6.95
E805   ESSLIN, MARTIN / Mediations: Essays on Brecht, Beckett, and the Media / $9.95
E820   GRAY, FRANCES / John Arden / $9.95
E695   HAYMAN, RONALD / How To Read A Play / $2.95
E796   HILTON, JULIAN / Georg Buchner / $8.95
E825   HUNTER, JIM / Tom Stoppard's Plays / $9.95
E795   PRONKO, LEONARD / Eugene Labiche and Georges Feydeau / $9.95
E798   SHANK, THEODORE / American Alternative Theater / $12.50

GROVE PRESS, INC., 196 West Houston St., New York, N.Y. 10014 ·